T0365967

I HUNG JESUS

I HUNG JESUS

A story based on the death of Jesus Christ as told through the eyes
of the TREE that became the implement of Jesus' death.

CARMINE LOMBARDO

ARCHWAY
PUBLISHING

Archway Publishing books may be ordered through booksellers or by contacting:

Archway Publishing
1663 Liberty Drive
Bloomington, IN 47403
www.archwaypublishing.com
844-669-3957

Interior Image Credit: Dorayne Lombardo

Scripture taken from the King James Version of the Bible.

ISBN: 978-1-6657-7022-4 (sc)
ISBN: 978-1-6657-7023-1 (e)

Library of Congress Control Number: 2024926169

Print information available on the last page.

Archway Publishing rev. date: 12/10/2024

"FOR GOD LOVED THE WORLD SO
MUCH THAT HE GAVE
HIS ONLY BEGOTTEN SON, IN ORDER THAT EVERYONE
EXERCISING FAITH IN HIM MIGHT NOT BE DESTROYED
BUT HAVE EVERLASTING LIFE." **John 3:16**

CONTENTS

Foreword ix

I Hung Jesus 1

Go! 9

How Strange 11

Jesus of Nazareth, King of the Jews! 14

Jesus, The Christ. 15

"He Is Innocent!" 17

Golgotha!. 21

But wait and watch. .23

King of Kings! Lord of Lords!. 25

Crash! 27

"Jesus of Nazareth, King of the Jews". 29

It Has Been Accomplished! 36

FOREWORD

Just two weeks ago I attended a concert at The Little Church Around The Corner on East 29th Street off of Fifth Avenue to hear my collaborator Bob Cohen's premiere for Basson. While there I stood mesmerized observing the incredible religious art work throughout the nave and chapels. I was moved beyond words. The exquisite expressive masterpieces in this historic garden church tucked away on the city streets of New York filled me soul with the sense of the Spirit at this season of Lent. Everything displayed there absorbed my life into the spirit of Christ's life and love.

And now your poem comes unexpectantly into my spirit at a very deep place in my contemplative moments. You wrote this many years ago. Its resurfacing, resulting in your sharing it with me, is in and of itself, a "resurrection" during this penitential time of 40 days till Easter. I am stunned by your work, your heart's expression, your souls struggle with the struggle of the passion and the gripping way you introduce the passion narrative of I HUNG JESUS. I am speechless.

This work is a classical piece, and channeled through the Spirit's leading, can ouch many lives. Let me spend concentrated time with it allowing it to wash over me with grace that carries me in the outpouring love of Christ's suffering as seen through the eyes of the tree. The scriptures refer to "trees of righteousness planted for the Glory of God." Your image of the tree is planted deeply in my heart and seared upon my prayerful reflections of your incredible use of words to bring us through your journey.

There is an oratorio here as well as an illustrated book.

What a blessing to read.

Thank you for your insights and for your revealing of your poetic heart.

-Ron W. Cadmus

I HUNG JESUS

The sun danced higher – hot that morn
And warmed my inner bones.
I yawned and stretched my sleepy arms
And twitched my toes on stones.

The carpet green around me
Blossomed golden hue,
While birds and bees and other trees
Busied themselves too.

The wind swam softly overhead,
Refreshing as it sprung,
Whirling, curling round about,
Kissing old and young

It was good to be alive,
To feel the surge and strength,
My bristling bark and tender leaves
Coming forth had meant

That Spring had come, a welcomed time
For nature, beast and man,
And God, creator of us all,
Blessed His master plan.

My life was easy, fixed in dirt,
Wholesome, fertile, brown,
And I became the pride and joy
Of all the trees around.

Far beyond there stood a wall,
A city painted white.
With streams of people to and fro,
It made a welcomed sight –
JERUSALEM, home of the Jews –

The name alone is ancient,
Their customs and their fears
Stemming back to Abraham,
Beyond a thousand years.

A solemn time, Passover Feast,
The Jews had come to know
An act of mercy shown by God
In Egypt long ago.

From distant lands far and near
They came in flooding tides.
The city bulged and groaned to breathe,
Hurting on all sides.

And then it happened; strange enough,
Soldiers flanked my hill,
Scanning through the countryside,
Their wagon empty still.

"What's this about?" I said in fear
As one stared straight at me,
And pointing with a mark of law,
He said, "That tree!"

My mind confused and gripped with pain,
Wild and hard to think,
Waited for the pointed ax
To strike its teeth and sink

Deep within my outer crust
And fibers to my bones.
Who would hear but only I,
My agony and groans.

I splattered bit by bit and then
My legs were torn apart.
Scattered on the carpet green,
The pounding of my heart

Sent me reeling round until
My body crashed and roared,
Thundering upon my hill –
Plucked and partly gored.

At their mercy there I lay,
A victim crushed by man,
Ready for the slaughter
Like a helpless lamb.

My arms, my arms were swished by strokes.
My hair leaves copped off clean.
All the pride I had was gone,
And what did it all mean?

They carried me with others too
And dumped us in their cart.
Crushed, I cried the burning tears
That filled my broken heart.

We clumped and bumped along the road
Until a halt was called,
Stopping in a courtyard where
The outer rim was walled.

Footsteps clamored heavy, close,
And then I saw this hand,
Hairy, huge, horrendous, hard,
Point in quick command –

"Take them; put them over there!"
He growled harsh and course.
Muscles bulging thick and firm,
His cat eyes spelled brute force.

He grabbed my arms and slammed me down
A table by his side,
And with an ax, cold and blunt,
Skinned me half alive.

I screamed! I cried for mercy"s sake,
But did he hear or care?
No, his heart was taught to kill
No matter who or where.

When I was through my body churned,
Punctured, crunched, complete,
Cut from end to end to show
Six inches by eleven feet.

Again, he picked me up and crashed me down,
Splintered, spliced, half dead,
Spinning to unconsciousness
When I hit my head.

The cool of the ev"ning woke me up.
The courtyard moonlight scene
Drenched me with the thought of what
Another day would mean.

But then I closed my eyes to sleep
Forgetting „bout the past.
Too hurt to move or even cry,
I slumbered deep and fast.

A shrill cry of the morning broke
The silence of the night,
A hand capped voice somewhere up high
Welcomed in the light.

The wind in whirlpools circled sand
And danced the wayward thorns –
Shadows, shields and tools of war,
Flags on poles and horns

Hanging on the wall around,
A fortress to behold
Of fighting men whose lust to kill
Was presently controlled.

My eyes sped side to side to see
Three pillars made of stone,
And each a ring of iron attached
Were signs of torture known.

Suddenly an angry cry
Thunder burst my ears,
"Away with him! Away with him!"
Bewildering my fears.

And then I saw him; I was touched.
His face was raw and sad,
Puffed with purple cheekbone welts,
A beard of blood he had.

A comic ruler robed in red,
They clothed him just for fun,
While his lips and muscles twitched,
Their play had just begun.

A soldier led him to the post,
Removed his robe and things,
And then his wrists above his head
Were tightened to the ring.

Quivering the man stood still
While soldiers came to see,
Waiting, watching, wondering,
Witnessing with me.

So many questions crossed my mind.
What did he do and say?
Why did they mock him as a king
And torture him this way?

A captain, young and colorful, Forwardly addressed
All the soldiers in the court
That the man confessed
-- He was a King! --
   King of the Jews!

Then laughter roared,
Because the soldiers knew
None was king but Caesar
And loyalty was due.

Soon the hateful, heartless one
Stomped upon the scene,
Bringing grins and shallow smiles,
Positions slightly leaned.

Closer, closer to the stone
He stalked to see the man,
And stepping back six feet behind
This weapon curled his hand –

Leather straps like octopus
Dangled on the stones,
Clad in clustered balls of lead
And strips of sharpened bones –

Waiting, waiting wantonly
For the captain"s sign,
Flashing, flipping, tearing deep,
Flesh to cut and grind –

GO!

Zip and zap the morsel flew
Crashing rib cage high.
The prisoner with knees collapsed
Gave a mournful cry.

A moment dull he straightened up.
The torture tool tore back.
With heavy rhythm full of pain,
It never let up slack.

The man's lips moved in trembling tides
As ruby drops of red
Trickled to the stones below
Draining him half dead.

Three minutes of that punishment
The pounding pain did swell.
He swayed unsteady, slumped and then
Uncontrolled, he fell.

Two soldiers came and freed his hands.
Cold water splashed his face.
His breath was shallow, swift and short
While others left their place.

Too weak to stand the prisoner
Sat and throbbed in pain,
And then the ones who left returned
Continuing their game.

The captain smiled and snickered.
Then nodding he agreed --
Party time to mock the King
Doing as they pleased.

They placed a scarlet robe on him,
And gave his hand a reed.
A crown of thorns they pressed on him
Which caused his head to bleed.

Trickling down his swollen cheeks
And matting in his beard,
Slapping, spitting, hitting him
They shouted and they jeered –

"Long live the King of the Jews!"
My heart went out to gentleness,
For not a word he said,
Cursed, condemned nor cried or wailed –
Such nobleness instead.

HOW STRANGE

Who was he?
A different kind of man.
The kind that draws respect and love
Even at the hand of his enemies.

When they finished with their game,
They helped him hobble by,
And then I found myself so moved,
My heart began to cry.

No sooner when they left, I heard
The anger of the crowd,
Shouting in re-echoed tones,
Piercing, pulsed and loud –

AWAY WITH HIM! KILL HIM! KILL HIM!

Three soldiers rushed and ran to us.
One strongly gripped my waist,
While others, two, along with me
Were taken in great haste.

The courtyard seared with faces,
Twisted, jarred, enraged,
Packed like jungle animals,
Unkempt, unfed and caged.

The governor, a stocky man,
Perplexed, yet aware,
Sat in nervous spasms on
A gold and scarlet chair.

His eyes were deep and troubled.
They sped from side to side.
He argued but the crowd of lust
For blood went simply wild.

The governor surrendered.
The merciless had won,
And with the washing of his hands,
He pleaded what was done –

"I am innocent of the blood of this just man!"

With unity and ill concerned
The hungry crowd returned –
"His blood be upon us and our children!"

"This is murder," I replied.
"The height of cruelty.
What"s said for man when he allows
Injustice to go free?"

And so, the robed one had to die.
The captain took his charge.
His name they printed on a board,
Bold, blunt, and large –

JESUS OF NAZARETH, KING OF THE JEWS!

A King beyond all time to come,
And Jesus was his name.
Where were all his followers
To help him in his claim?

"What sort of King are you, my friend?"
I asked myself to find
The answer from my younger days
And inroads of my mind,

When older folks, my fellow trees,
Had told the story of
This King, who born with righteousness,
Was sacrificed for love.

Delivering the world to truth
And perfect harmony,
Paying for the sins of man,
And this was he –

JESUS, THE CHRIST

Oh, my Jesus, even I,
For all the years I grew.
Even I, a wretched one,
Would hang and torture you.

"No! No!" I cried.
It was beyond belief
For me to be the instrument
To cause him all that grief.

My Lord, forgive me!

They fetched two others from a cell
And shoved them both in line.
With soldiers blocked and bearing spears,
They waited for the sign.

All was ready but my part,
The part that I would play.
Then on his shoulders holding firm
He gasped and made his way.

Slowly, slowly, weak and weary,
He bent and made his way.

Clusters gathered everywhere –
Windows, roofs and walls,
Prying, pushing, pressing in,
Crying out in calls –

"HE IS INNOCENT!"

Women veiled their eyes from sight.
Others held their breasts.
Some would turn their heads and cry
And openly confessed their love for him.

One was small and gentle,
And neatly dressed in black.
Standing near among them all,
Her eyes beheld the fact

That all that precious love she knew
Was now condemned to die.
A sword of sorrow pierced her heart –
Her eyes to dry to cry –

His mother.

His body drenched,
I could tell, Bedraggled, bent and low,
Dripping blood and weaker still
He wobbled to and fro.

Holding on to all he had
Which drained his very soul,
And falling, falling to the dust,
Dropped me uncontrolled.

We were at the marketplace,
The bottom of the hill.
The captain rushed and looking on
Saw him lying still.

Blood flowed freely from his crown,
New and beaded red.
For him to carry on
Was foolish so instead

The captain searched the crowd and saw
A heavy muscled man,
And pointing power to his eyes,
Gave a quick command –

"You! You, there! Carry this for him!"
With tightened, firm and cursing lips,
He picked me as a limb.

Jesus still lay gasping,
But I was glad to see
At least he had a little help
To bear the weight of me.

The captain reached and picked him up
While nothing more was said,
And so, he staggered step by step,
Loose with lowered head.

We turned and met some women
Moved deeply by his sight,
Crying, craving helping hands
To help him in his plight.

He stopped and looked, compassionate,
And slowly turned his head,
Putting effort in his words,
He grasped his hands and said,

"Daughters of Jerusalem,
Weep not for me.
Weep for your children
For a time will see
People saying, „You're barren blessed.
Your womb not born

Of children nursing breasts,
For the mountains they will cry
Fall on us and the hills nearby
Bury us.'""

The captain reared and running,
Rushed the slight delay,
And pressing forth the column moved
Drudgingly its way.

"Back! Back! Let us through!
Move on!" the soldiers balked,
Prodding weary prisoners,
Stumbling as they walked.

Out the gate and thirty yards
Up a rocky mound,
Dark and dreary, dreadful, eerie,
Marked with death abound –

GOLGOTHA!

The captain called us to a halt.
An ordered line was made,
Letting only few come through
To see a debt be paid.

Flowers grew beyond the rim,
Pink, white and red,
And northwest „bout a hundred feet,
A tomb to lay the dead.

The man who carried me stood still
And laid me by his side,
But deep compassion in his eyes
Could not be denied

That he was moved by Jesus,
Complete with captured heart,
And walking slowly bowed his head
Away in sad depart.

His mother and a young lad dear
Came speechless up the hill.
With outstretched hands her lily cheeks
Flowed tender tears at will.

Others followed in the stream,
The ones who loved him too,
Humble, helpless, hurting hearts
With nothing they could do

BUT WAIT AND WATCH

He begged them not to cry for him,
To show their strength in prayer,
But could they help their feelings full
Of pain and despair?
No, they were human too.

The captain gave the order,
And Jesus was the first,
A lowly thief began to cowl
And howl with sudden bursts.

He cried, "I didn"t do a thing."
"Don"t tell me, man." a soldier scorned,
"Tell it to the King."

The quiet thief beside him
Proved pensive standing there,
Folding hands and thoughtful eyes
Pictured him in prayer.

Two priests among the silent crowd
Waited with a smirk,
To save a nation for one man,
They schemed the dirty work.

Four soldiers manned each prisoner
While people pressed and pressed.
"Get back! Get back! Get back you fools!"
The captain''s soldiers stressed.

A woman ran and holding out
Within her hands a flask,
Drink, please drink and ease the pain,
Her pleading eyes had asked.

But he refused to take a drink
To ease the searing pain,
Taking full the sacrifice
With honor to his name –

KING OF KINGS!
LORD OF LORDS!

Moving in the soldiers stripped
Garments, sandals, all,
And wrapping cloth around his loins
Readied for his fall.

The sun was climbing in the sky,
And stretched behind I lay,
While cruel, so cruel the hated one
Forced his evil way,

And grabbing Jesus" arms full back,
Brought him to the ground.
Thorns and thistles tore in him
When he hit the mound
Jesus groaned but nothing more
While soldiers held him firm,
Ready for the final blows
To puncture, pierce and burn.

At that moment I was lost,
A pit of anguish too.
Help me, Lord, I"m weak, I pray.
I need the strength of you.

And then within me courage came,
A faith beyond my own.
With inner hope and trust I knew
We weren"t there alone –

Yes, by the grace of God I knew
We weren"t there alone.

The evil one positioned
With square nails in his mouth,
And taking one felt Jesus" wrist
And hammered with a clout –

CRASH!

Plunging deep in flesh and me,
The nails held us in pain --
Pulsing in vibrating tones,
Proceeding with the same
Until all was done.

Drops of blood and drops of sweat
Trickled down my side,
But not a word or mere complaint
Was heard or even cried.

His mother fainted falling back
When the deed was done,
And full compassion from the lad
Took her from her son.

The hated one moved back and raised
His arms in signaled tones
While Jesus quivered, writhed in pain
Again, in murmured groans.

Soldiers lifted higher still,
Ker plunk I fell in place,
Jerked and jarred and firmly set
To finalize the case.

Compassion knows no hatred,
And to his lips a prayer,
A prayer said for the soldiers
Whose law had brought them there –

"Father, please forgive them,
For they know not what they do."

A ladder on my neck,
I held the evil one,
While he nailed a sign to tell
The crime of God"s own Son –

"JESUS OF NAZARETH, KING OF THE JEWS"

In Hebrew, Latin, Greek,
A name for all the world to seek.

Done, he went to do his deed.
The other two were fast --
A painting of three figures who
Would forever last
In the hearts of multitudes.

My cup was full and over.
I couldn"t bear to see,
To hear and feel the pulsing pain,
My Lord hung on me –

The pulsing, punctured, piercing pain
My Lord hung on me.

I wondered. How I wondered
With time grinding slow.

Time, you stealer, friend of death,
Even you don''t know
The will of his Father –
How long it will last.

Unbearable he strained himself
To raise his bleeding feet,
Knotted muscle, forearm cramps,
Breathing incomplete.

Drawing air but no exhale
Excruciating too,
Body sudden jumps and jars
Repeated through and through.

Sagging deeper, deeper still
And hanging from his wrists,
While the elders and the priests
Pointed shaking fists,

Scourging vengeance from their lips,
Glad to see him die,
Asking questions, time again,
Tell me, tell me why –

"You are the one that can pull down the sanctuary and
lift it up in three days," Ha!
Another says:
"If you are the Son of God, come down."
"He helped others; he cannot help himself."
"Give us a sign."

But lo, the sign was given.
Now silence left its mark,
With time of justice soon to fall
Upon them and embark

All their evil selfish pride,
Hypocrites and hounds,
Hardened, dark and dreadful hearts
Ever to be found.

Midday and a darkness fell,
Deeper, deeper blue,
While the sun, the heaven"s lamp,
Hid his face from view.

For where his Lord hung in shame,
Sickened, sorry sight.
He couldn"t bear to look upon
The spot and shine its light.
Strange, strange happening.

At that time, the soldiers had
Their midday rations break,
Drank their wine and toasted to
The health of my Lord"s sake.

The captain bent and grabbed his robe,
Tossing it away,
And rolling bones the soldiers took
The seamless robe in play.

My eyes turned for a second.
His mother closer came,
Broken hearted, drawn and pale,
The mercy and the pain

Looked at him hanging there,
A moment, two,
While the lad in comfort led
His mother from the view.

Tighter, tighter – breaking point,
His muscles jerked and wound,
When the robber on his left
Jeered in angry sound –
"Are you the Messiah?
Save yourself and us!"

But the robber on his right
Lifted hard and said,
"Do you not fear God
Condemned the life we led?
Justly we receive reward
Due to us so long,
But this man has done no wrong."

Then sinking lower in his pit
O pain and sorrow too,
Took one breath and spoke these words –
Within his heart he knew –

"Jesus, remember me when you come into your kingdom."

Forgiveness he was asking and
Pure melody returned.
Full of love, compassion for
The sinner who had yearned
For mercy.
"Verily I say unto you today,
You shall be with me in paradise."
I was overjoyed, overjoyed
For all the suffering done,

Love was conqueror of sin –
The ransom of the Son of God.

Hope for man"s redemption
And glory be fulfilled,
His final hours closing in
Drew breathing painful still.

Burning, burning mouth and throat,
He groaned and asked for drink,
While deeper, deeper into shock
His body slipped to sink,

But then he looked and nodded to
The lad who standing by
Moved to bring his mother near
Too crushed with hurt to cry.

He clenched his teeth against the pain
And straightened knees to breathe.
Then humbly with a voice of love
He bequeathed:

"Mother, behold your son."
And to the lad,
"Son, behold your mother."

Slowly turned they walked away
With understanding hearts,
While chills and shocks of death beheld
His struggling lips impart,

"My God! My God! Why have you forsaken me?"

Gleeful eyes the enemy
Had thought he called for aid.
Happy hoping him a hoax
A penalty he paid for being an imposter.

"I thirst!"

A plaintive plea, a soldier held
A sponge of sour wine,
But when it touched his swollen lips,
It dripped away declined.

Three o" clock his stricken lungs
Heavy heaved and cried,

"Father, into thy hands I commit my spirit.

IT HAS BEEN ACCOMPLISHED!

Sagging slowly, resting head
To his right he died.

A soldier came and pierced his side,
And blood and water spout.
Drops of blood and sacrifice,
A broken heart poured out.

Then rolls of rattling thunder roared,
Flashing lightning near,
Wrenching, rocking, rolling earth,
Beating breasts in fear.

Coming forth the captain said
A most astounding line.
Though pagan in his ways,
He knew at that time –

"Truly, this was the Son of God!"

When they came to take him,
Saddened was my heart –
Naked, bold against the sky
I had played my part,

But sanctified with blessed hope,
My master took his call,
And by the blood of Jesus Christ
Redemption came for all!

ALLELUIA! ALLELUIA! ALLELUIA!

God love you,
Carmine

Printed in the United States
by Baker & Taylor Publisher Services